THE LORD'S PRAYER

A DEVOTIONAL

A DEVOTIONAL AND SPIRITUAL THOUGHTS BOOK

BY ANNALETA ELAINE SWANN

THE LORD'S PRAYER

Swann Orchid Publishing Company
Nassau, Bahamas

First Edition

ISBN: 9781790970452

Printed in the United States of America

DEDICATION

To my grandchildren – Phillip Eric, Ashanti, and Noah. Know that God's Hand is upon your lives as He seeks ways to use you for His Honour and Glory

Contents

PREFACE

As an educator of many decades' experience, I have always been cognizant of my role in and ability to positively influence the children who were placed under my care. As a primary school teacher, I taught all subjects, including religious studies. As I taught my classes, and prepared them for presentations at general school assemblies and special occasions, I was always careful to include opportunities and invitations for individuals to begin a personal relationship with Jesus Christ – the Son of God.

These experiences sensitized the need for exploring new avenues to spreading the word of God, while creating new tools to help individuals understand some of the more difficult aspects of the study of the scriptures. My first ventures into writing however, came by accident. My personal exploration of the Holy Scriptures provided an opportunity to create short summaries and expositions which has been collated to form the first series of books.

It is hoped that this series of books first book begins to meet this objective, and that as you read, you are refreshed and blessed in your spiritual sojourn, and spurred as well to conduct your own in-depth search and review of the Holy Scriptures.

FOREWORD

God knows who to entrust with the exposition and the devotional application of His Word. He has found such a person in our sister, Annaleta Elaine Swann. Her treatise of the Lord's "model prayer" is most insightful. I have been very enlightened and blessed.

Sister Swann's academic background qualified her for proper research, and her years of spiritual preparation by God for such a ministry to us. Reading it will prove a great blessing to you, and all whom it may be share with.

Therefore, I take pleasure in my recommendation to you for profitable reading and meditation.

Evangelist Thomas (Tom) H. Roberts, JP, OBE.

Pastor Emeritus,

East Street Gospel Chapel

Nassau, Bahamas

ACKNOWLEDGEMENTS

Expressions of gratitude are extended to the pastors, leaders and membership of Freeport Gospel Chapel who form my spiritual family and support network. Additionally, I would like to thank my children who encouraged me and provided the avenue with which to publish these series of books.

Foundational thoughts on An Exposition on the Laws of God were inspired by presentations on Psalm 19 by Senior Pastor Hartley Thompson and the late Deacon Carl Sweeting of Freeport Gospel Chapel, Freeport, Bahamas.

Summary

I have divided this model of The Lord's Prayer into an Introduction, Five Petitions, and a Doxology. Most fascinating to me is the fact that each Petition is continually explained throughout the Scriptures. It is no small wonder that Jesus says to His disciples in St. John 5:39, *"Search the Scriptures; for in them ye think you have eternal life: and they are they which testify of Me."*

I have used only a few of the many Scripture verses that could be utilized to complement each Petition. At the end, I combined the short introduction with the doxology to complete this portion of my exposition.

Introduction: Our Father Who Art In Heaven Hallowed Be Thy Name

Corresponding verses

    a. *"The Heaven, even the Heavens are the Lord's."* *Psalms115:16*

    b. *"Thou art holy. O Thou that inhabitest the praises of Israel."* *Psalm 22:3*

Petition 1: Thy Kingdom Come

Corresponding verses

    a. *"Thy throne O God is forever."* *Hebrews 1: 8*

    b. *"Thy Kingdom is an Everlasting Kingdom."* *Psalm 143:13*

Petition 2: Thy will be done on earth as it is in Heaven.

Corresponding verses

    a. *"I delight to do Thy Will O my God."* *Psalm 40: 8*

    b. *"That ye may stand perfect and complete in all the will of God."* *Colossians 4:12*

Petition 3: Give us this day our daily bread.

Corresponding verses

    a.   *What is 'Our Daily Bread'?*

    b.   *"I am the Bread of Life." St. John 6:48*

Petition 4: Forgive us our debts as we forgive our debtors.

Corresponding verses

    a.   *"Who can forgive sins, but God only?" Mark 2:7*

    b.   *"The Son of Man hath power on earth to forgive sins." Mark 2:10*

Petition 5: Lead us not into temptation but deliver us from evil.

Corresponding verses

    a.   *"God who is faithful, will not suffer you to be tempted above that ye are able." 1 Corinthians 10:13*

    b.   *"The Lord our God shall deliver us." 2 Chronicles 32:11*

Doxology: For thine is the Kingdom, and Power, and Glory.

Corresponding verse

    a.   *"Worthy is the lamb that was slain to receive power, and riches, and wisdom, and strength and honour, and glory, and blessing." Revelation 5:12*

Conclusion: Amen

Introduction

Our Father, Who Art In Heaven

The Way of Salvation is not specifically dealt with in this modeled prayer. What really amazes me about this prayer, is that many times it is used universally in congregations consisting of Christians and non- Christians. Obviously, during these occasions we do not remember that this prayer was given as a model or pattern to the disciples and by extension to all believers, not to unbelievers. They do not have the esteemed privilege to refer to God as their Father.

The disciples were obviously interested in knowing how to pray. So the Lord Jesus began with 'Our'. In St. John 6:68-71 Peter confessed on behalf of all the disciples, except Judas, that Jesus had the words of eternal life and that they believed that He was the Son of God. Therefore, God was their Father.

The following episode describes another time when the disciples acknowledged Jesus as the Son of God. After the feeding the 5 000 as recorded in the Gospels of St. Matthew, Mark, and John; the Lord Jesus, realizing that His disciples were tired, told them to get into the boat and sail across to the other side of the lake (Sea of Galilee), while He went up to the mountain to pray. While He was away from them, between the hours of 3 am and 6 am, a very violent storm arose. (St. Matthew 14:23-24.)

Among this company of men there were fishermen who once earned their livelihood by fishing daily in these waters; there were others who may have frequented the coastlines, or worked in the fertile fields nearby. No doubt, these men were accustomed to the storms that sometimes seemed to arise out of nowhere in this area. But this one was different! Strong winds blew the clouds furiously across the firmament; streaks of lightening flashed fiercely across the sky; thunders roared excessively loud; rain poured down in torrents. Even the seafaring men among the disciples were greatly afraid.

As the disciples feared for their lives, because of the raging waves, they beheld, what appeared to be, an apparition walking on the stormy sea. They were horrified! They cried out in fear. As usual, our Divine Rescuer who is never farther than a whisper away from His own heard their cry. I can image Him smiling to Himself as He thought 'what would these do when I go away from them?' However, He, is omniscient, and knew that the Father would send the Holy Spirit to be with them. He identified Himself, and they are comforted. Oh! what a word. Jesus identified Himself. Hallelujah!

Jesus continues to identify Himself! I am certain that many times when we as believers cry out to the Lord Jesus, our Saviour and Friend, He reminds us that He is always there; even when things appear to go wrong and the storms of life hide Him from our view. As soon as the Lord Jesus entered the ship, with Peter, the storm ceased. St. Matthew 14:33 records: And they that were in the ship came and worshipped Him saying, "Of a truth thou art the Son of God."

The Lord Jesus knew the hearts of His chosen disciples. They did not go away when the others did. He knew that they were eager to know more about Him. They really wanted to know how to pray. He did not have to refer them to Psalm 66:18 which says, "If I regard iniquity in my heart, the Lord will not hear me." They were eager to learn the Truth, so the Omniscient One did not draw their attention to Proverbs 28: 9, "He that turneth away his heart from hearing the law, even his prayer shall be an abomination." (St. John 6:67-69.) Obviously, they loved to hear God's word. I am sure that being in the company of the Son of God, gave them a peace that they could not find anywhere else. Certainly, their prayer would not have been an abomination.

Our Redeemer identified Himself with His disciples when he said 'our Father'. In His High priestly prayer, (St. John17:1-26), our Intercessor says in verses 9-10, "I pray for them (His disciples), I pray not for the world, but for them which Thou hast given me; for they are Thine. And all Mine are Thine, and Thine are Mine; and I am glorified in them." The words 'them which thou hast given me' acknowledged their connection with an all-sufficient heavenly Father, through the Lord Jesus Christ.

In verses 20-21, He says, "Neither pray I for these alone but for them which shall believe on me through their (the disciples') word (which is really the Word of God). That they all may be one; as Thou Father, art in me, and I in Thee, that they also may be one in us." Verse

21 includes all believers down through the ages, the other sheep that were not a part of the fold at that time. I was as a worm in the sight of a Most Holy God before His Beloved Son snatched me from a burning Hell.

In these two words, OUR FATHER, the redeemed are given an enormous privilege. The Lord Jesus could have said Our Heavenly Father, but in this awesome approach, to Holy Deity, He describes the love of an Almighty God for an undeserved frail human race. He assumes responsibility for our disobedience and gives all who believe on Him the privilege to boldly approach the throne of grace addressing God through His name as Our Father who art in Heaven. Praise be to God! By His death on the Cross of Calvary and His resurrection, Our Lord and Saviour, Jesus Christ, connects all believers with a God who is Great, High, and Holy.

How can a God of such lofty magnitude condescend to my low estate to become 'my Father'! This is a mystery that I can neither understand nor comprehend! Bowing humbly before Him, with the hymn writer, Elizabeth C. Clephane in the hymn 'Beneath the Cross of Jesus', I admit that

'From my smitten heart with tears,

Two wonders I confess.

The wonders of Thy Glorious Love,

And my own worthlessness.'

Hallowed Be Thy Name.

Very early in this modeled prayer, commonly called "The Lord's Prayer", the Lord Jesus demands that God's name be hallowed. That is, that it must be regarded as Holy, consecrated, and sanctified: completely set apart from all other names in heaven and on earth. In 1 Chronicles 29:13, God says that His name is "Glorious". In Exodus 20:5, God describes Himself as being a jealous God. Therefore, because of His jealousy, He will not give His Glory to another. The Psalmist David speaks about God's holy hands, His holy hill, and His holy promises as well as other aspects of His holiness. All of God's Divine characteristics are Holy. In fact, God is the personification of Holiness. In the Old Testament those who disdained His holiness, in spite of the fact that they meant well, were severely punished.

The following abstract is taken from <u>The Holiness of God</u> by Bob Deffenbaugh from a series called <u>Let Me See Thy Glory.</u>

"Not recognizing God's Holiness is being irreverent. God takes this very seriously. Even when our motives are sincere, and we are actively involved in worshipping God, we must constantly remind ourselves of the holiness of God and maintain a reverence for Him according to His instructions."

The prophet Isaiah saw seraphim worshipping El-Elyon - the Almighty God - as they sang "Holy, Holy, Holy is The Lord of Hosts; the earth is full of his Glory." God's Son, the Lord Jesus Christ, referred to God as His Holy Father in His high priestly Prayer in St. John17:11. Revelation 4:8 says that the four beasts continually praise God saying, ""Holy, Holy, Holy, Lord God Almighty, which was, and is, and is to come."

Archbishop of Canterbury, Rowan Williams, sums up a tribute to The Most High God by saying; ***"understand what you are talking about: the Holiness of Almighty God."*** We should also understand who we are talking about: A thrice Holy God." (Isaiah 6:3.) Continuing his summary, the Archbishop says that this is serious business; that it is a most wonderful, yet frightening reality: one that we as finite beings can never imagine.

Finally, as I complete this section of my thesis, I am cognizant of the fact that with my finite mind, I am not worthy to describe a Holy Triune God; therefore, it is with great humility that I ascribe these few attributes to Our Heavenly Father; all taken from His Holy, inspired Word.

(a) God is the <u>Ancient of Days</u> and the Giver of eternal life. Daniel 27:21; St. John 17:2

(b) God, the Creator, is <u>Blessed</u> forevermore. Bless His Holy Name. Romans 1:25; Psalm 103:1

(c) God's love never <u>changes:</u> all who believe in Him has everlasting life. Malachi 3: 6; St. John 3:16

(d) God's name is <u>dreadful among unbelievers.</u> All nations before him are counted less than nothing. Malachi 1:14; Isaiah 40:17

(e) God gives His own, <u>everlasting</u> strength. His mercy is from everlasting to everlasting upon them that fear Him. Isaiah 26:4; Psalm 103:17

(f) God is <u>Faithful:</u> He will keep his covenant with Israel. Isaiah 33:17; Hosea 14:9

(g) God is <u>Gracious:</u> He gives grace and glory to them that walk uprightly. 1 Peter 2:3; Psalm 84:11

(h) God's name is <u>Holy:</u> It must not be profaned nor blasphemed. Psalm111:9; Matthew 6:9

(i) God is Eternal, <u>Immortal,</u> and Invisible: He is the only wise God. Give Him the honour that is due to Him. 1 Timothy 1:17; 1 Timothy 6;1

(j) The Lord Thy God is a <u>Jealous God:</u> be mindful of Him that sustains thee. Exodus 20:5;   Deuteronomy 32:18

(k) God is thy <u>keeper.</u> He will keep in perfect peace those who trust in Him. Psalm 121:5; Isaiah 26:3

(l) The Lord God is our <u>Light</u> and our salvation. Let us reflect that light in a sin darkened world. Psalm 27:1; St. Matthew 5:16

(m) God is awesome in <u>majesty,</u> excellent in power, and just in judgment. He is worthy to be praised. Job 27:23; Zechariah 9:9

(n) God is our <u>nourisher:</u> He feeds us with the Bread of Life and satisfies our thirst with the living Water of His word. Isaiah 1:2; St. John 4:14

(o) God is <u>Omnipotent.</u> He is worthy to receive all glory, honour, and praise.   Jude1:25; Revelation 19:6; Malachi 1:14; 1 Timothy 6:16

(p) God is Everlasting: His love abideth forever. Isaiah 40:28; 1 Peter 1:23

(q) God is faithful: He will keep his covenant with Israel. Jeremiah 33:17; Jeremiah 46: 27

(r) God is a Deliverer: He delivereth the righteous out of all his troubles. Psalm 34:7; Daniel 6:7

PETITION 1:

THY KINGDOM COME

Corresponding verses

(a) *"Thy throne O God is forever." Hebrews 1: 8*

(b) *"Thy Kingdom is an Everlasting Kingdom." Psalm 143:13*

I will begin this section with a few excerpts directly from the Word of God.

"For the Kingdom of God is not meat and drink; but righteousness, and peace, and joy in the Holy Ghost." Romans 14:17.

"The Lord hath prepared His throne in the heavens; and His kingdom ruleth over all." Psalm 103:19.

"How great are His signs! His kingdom is an everlasting kingdom, and His dominion is from generation to generation." Daniel 4:3

"Thy throne O God is forever and ever: a scepter of Righteousness is the scepter of Thy kingdom." Hebrews 1:8

A kingdom may be defined as a nation or state ruled by a king or queen or, a sphere in which certain conditions prevail. During Our Lord's physical sojourn on earth He had an overwhelming passion for the Kingdom of God. According to His recorded ministry it seems as if He did not mention His own glorious millennium reign as much as He spoke about the blessings of those who would become citizens of the Kingdom of God.

According to early Bible translators, although the Lord Jesus used both terms: The Kingdom of God and The kingdom of heaven, very seldom did He use them interchangeably. Nonetheless, the use of these terms could be attributed to the original translators. St, Mark, St. Luke, and St. John, referred to this Spiritual domain as 'The Kingdom of God'; whereas, St. Matthew referred to it as 'The Kingdom of Heaven.' Bible scholars believe that Matthew used the latter because his writing was primarily for the Jews. Although the majority of the Jewish rulers had very little regard for God's Son, The Lord Jesus, they reverenced Jehovah very highly and used His name very sparingly. That being said, the inscription above Our Saviour's head at His crucifixion left no room for doubt. Through the intervention of the Holy Spirit, the proclamation was written in Hebrew, Greek and Latin: This is Jesus: The King of the Jews. The Jewish authorities may have thought that this was in mockery but, in truth, this superscription was a testimony, as well as a prophecy. In due time, Jesus, as King, would be the ruler of all kingdoms of this world inclusive of Jewry. Isaac Watts (1674-1748), in conjunction with Psalm 72, wrote the following stanza:

Jesus shall reign where'er the sun

Does his successive journeys run;

His Kingdom spread from shore to shore,

Till moons shall wax and wane no more.

What Constitutes A Kingdom?

For this purpose, I am defining the main parts of a kingdom as a king, or queen, and its citizens. Within the kingdom there must be some form of communication between the ruler and his subjects: the citizens; hence the need to establish Laws and a Government. (In The Kingdom of God, the Laws are The Word of God. The Government will be upon the shoulders of The Lord Jesus Christ who is the King of Glory.)

At present, the rulers of this world are at their wits' end trying to choose the most appropriate type of government for their citizens and their territories: a type of government that will solve all the problems of every country. All forms of government will fade into obscurity whether it be a democracy, an aristocratic government, or a dictatorship. Only the theocratic government that will be established by Jehovah Himself will solve all the problems of humanity, once and for all.

What Is The Kingdom of God?

In the Moody handbook of Theology, Paul Enns defines The Kingdom of God as, The rule of The Eternal Sovereign God over all creation and all things both in heaven and on earth. Psalm 103:19 reads – "The Lord hath prepared His throne in the heavens; and His Kingdom rules over all." Daniel 4:3 states "How great are His (God's) signs! and how mighty are the wonders! His kingdom is an everlasting kingdom, and His dominion is from generation to generation." However, the author continues and adds that "The Kingdom of God is the sphere of salvation that one enters into at the new birth."

As Christians, we became citizens of The Kingdom of God through the new birth or being born again of the Holy Spirit. (St. John 3:1-18.) In this context, the Kingdom of God is comprised of all mankind that willingly submit to God. No one will be able to pluck us out of this Kingdom. We will be with Christ far above all principality,

and power, and might, and dominion, and every name that is named...'
Ephesians 1:21. The rest of creation will be destroyed.

The account of The Rich Young Ruler as recorded in St. Mark chapter 10 says that the young man went away sad because he had great possessions. I believe Jesus was sad also. St. Mark says that as soon as Jesus looked on him, even before the young ruler spoke, Jesus loved him. Being a ruler among the Jews, this young man was acquainted with the Torah. Therefore, he knew the Commandments. The Lord Jesus saw that this man had Spiritual potentiality. He was well equipped, academically, to enter the Kingdom of God. He would have fit quite nicely into that little flock to whom the Father would give the Kingdom, a Kingdom of real love, joy, peace, and lasting prosperity. A Kingdom that the young ruler disdained for the beggarly elements of this world; he had hidden the word in his heart but he did not apply his heart unto wisdom and subsequently sinned against God.

I believe that it was with great passion that Jesus uttered these three words as He taught His disciples how to pray. He knew what was in store for the whole world. He looked ahead through the corridors of Time and envisioned the suffering of His people the Jews; He saw the trials and tribulations that His present-day followers would face; and He knew that apostasy would raise its ugly head. As He spoke to the Jewish multitude in St. John 10:16, Jesus mentioned us, the Gentiles, although we were not 'sheep of His fold' at that time.

He also prayed for us in His high priestly prayer to His Father in St. John chapter 17.

How Do Members Of The Universe Become Citizens Of The Kingdom Of God?

According to St. John 3:3 & 7 no one becomes a citizen of the Kingdom of God by natural birth. "Jesus answered and said unto him, "Verily, verily, I say unto thee, except a man be born again, he cannot see the kingdom of God. Marvel not that I said unto thee, Ye must be born again."

Here are three methods which are all one of the same.

1. We become citizens of the Kingdom of God through the New Birth. St. John 3:18.

2. We become citizens of the Kingdom of God by Naturalization. Ephesians 2:19

3. We become citizens of the Kingdom of God through the granting of an Amnesty. Galatians 5:1.

During His discourse with Nicodemus, Our Lord Jesus explained quite vividly the heavenly and earthly connotations of a Spiritual and a natural birth. Bear with me as I attempt to explain, with the guidance of the Holy Spirit, the concepts of interpretations of the 'New Birth' and the birth into the Kingdom of God through Naturalization and by Amnesty.

1. <u>The New Birth: What does it Mean?</u>

During Nicodemus' encounter with Jesus in St. John 3: 1-21, Nicodemus was puzzled when Jesus mentioned the New Birth. Jesus was surprised and told him that, as a teacher in Israel, he should have known those things. In fact, it is believed that Nicodemus was a member of the highest religious group in Jerusalem and should have studied the relationship of Father and Son between God the Father and His people Israel.

Although 'born again' is not mentioned among the prophecies, to become sons of their Father God, the Israelites were, as it were 'born again' or born the second time. In Deuteronomy 32, Moses, by revelation and inspiration of the Holy Spirit, spoke of the Lord God as their Father who had bought them to be His children (sons and daughters). In Jeremiah 31:9 God declares Himself as a Father to Israel and claimed Ephraim as His first born among the children of Israel. For the length of time Jesus took to explain the New Birth to Nicodemus, it appears as if the teaching in Deuteronomy 32 and Jeremiah 31 were 'foreign' to him.

However, the Lord Jesus gradually impressed upon the heart of Nicodemus the need to be knowledgeable about the Kingdom of God. In St. John 3:3, He said, "Verily, verily I say unto thee except a man be born again, he cannot see the Kingdom of God."

A few minutes later in answer to Nicodemus's statement of this act being unrealistic, Jesus answered, "Verily, verily I say unto thee, except a man be born of the water and of the Spirit, he CANNOT ENTER into the Kingdom of God." Nicodemus, being recognized by his colleagues as a Master Teacher of Israel, was greatly puzzled in so much, that as Jesus continued His discourse, He said emphatically, "Marvel not that I said unto thee, YE MUST BE BORN AGAIN."

A few of the divinely inspired prophets including David, Isaiah, and Daniel spoke of a kingdom over which God would be the absolute ruler, but in the Old Testament there is no clear explanation of how one might enter this kingdom. However, during this dispensation of Grace, the Holy Spirit has written this story on the hearts of believers and non-believers alike in such a manner that John 3:16 is the most popular memorized Scripture verse in Christian countries.

In his article entitled 'What does the Bible say about the New Birth?' Jack Zavada - a Bible scholar says that our Lord Jesus breaks down His discourse with Nicodemus into answering the following questions:

a.   What is the New Birth?

b.   How is the New Birth realised?

Kindly bear with me, my dear reader, as I by the grace of God, the Holy Spirit, and the power of His Word that works in me, humbly endeavour to answer these questions according to Holy Scriptures.

a.   *What is the New Birth?*

According to Romans 3:21-26, we were all humanly born into sin. God has made this provision (The New Birth) for 'whosoever will' through the sacrifice of His Son Jesus Christ who has redeemed us once for all: our hands have been made clean and more importantly, our hearts have been made pure not because of any good that we have done; for while we were still in our accursed condition, under God's recommendation, Christ died for us.

1 Peter 1:3-14 assures us that because God - The Father in His

great mercy has given us a new birth into a living hope through the resurrection of Jesus Christ from the dead, we have an inheritance that can never perish; it is reserved in heaven for us.

In 2 Corinthians 5, St. Paul writes: If anyone is in Christ, he is a new creation. Simply put "the New Birth is entrance into the Kingdom of God."

b.   *How is the New Birth realised?*

God gives us this New Birth. It cannot be obtained. It has been undeservedly bestowed upon us. Christ in His own body bore our sins that we through His death may believe on Him and receive the righteousness of God: righteousness and blessings from the God of our salvation. Hallelujah!

The admonition given to Nicodemus over two thousand years ago still applies today. In order to enter the Kingdom of God You must be born again. A good understanding of the New Life can be obtained by asking the Holy Spirit to illuminate your mind as you read, study, and meditate on St. John chapter 3.

Below is a short exhortation based mainly on verses 10- 18 of St. John 3. Kindly consider it for your personal spiritual gratification.

With due respect to the Triune God, under His divine guidance, this question will be answered directly from Holy Scripture. However, these are only a few of the privileges we will enjoy.

i.   After we have received the New Birth our names will be written in heaven. St. Luke 10:20.

ii.   Immediately, we will seek first the Kingdom of

heaven. St. Matthew 6:33.

iii.   Having submit ourselves seriously unto God, we will receive power to resist the devil. James 4:7.

iv.   We will not speak evil of one another. James 4:11.

v.   We will be led by the Holy Spirit and walking in it, we will obey its prompting and produce the fruit of love, joy, peace, longsuffering, gentleness, goodness, faith, meekness, and self-control.

vi.   We will continue to ask God for His grace to LIVE in the Spirit. Galatians 5:25.

vii.   As ambassadors for Christ, we not only tell others about His goodness, but we will plead with those who are rebellious to become reconciled to Him. 2 Corinthians 5:20.

viii.   We will endure hardships especially for the sake of the Gospel and will strive with the help of the Holy Spirit to be a good soldier of our Lord and Saviour Jesus Christ. 2 Timothy 2:3

ix.   Finally, we will acknowledge our faults one to another and like the saints of the Old and New Testaments, ask God to forgive us when we 'mess up' or sin against Him.

2. <u>Naturalization</u>

Gregg Morrison defines naturalization as a process by which the Government of the United States of America, confers citizenship upon a foreign citizen or national after he/she fulfils the requirements established by Congress. Therefore, naturalization is the act of being politically accepted as a citizen of a country in which a person has resided for a prescribed length of time. The applicant cannot be an alien or total stranger when he applies for citizenship. Once the privilege has been granted, he must take a pledge of allegiance to respect and honour the laws of his/her new country. He is no longer an alien, but is entitled to the rights and privileges of naturally born citizens of that country. However, as stated above there are no naturally born citizens in the Kingdom of God. Romans 3:10-18.

Take a closer look with me at two points from this definition with a Scriptural prospective.

a. *We are politically accepted by the King of kings as a citizen of the Kingdom of God.*

The way to Salvation as explained by our Lord and Saviour Jesus Christ to Nicodemus, may seem rather cheap at first sight. However, the term, 'The Son of Man must be lifted up', is included. This refers to our Saviour's vicarious death on the cross of Calvary for us as hell- deserving sinners; our redemption, and ultimately, our entrance into the Kingdom of God! As clearly stated by our Lord Jesus Christ Himself and throughout the Epistles, this is NOT A CHEAP WAY TO ESCAPE DAMNATION INTO HELL! In fact, our purpose should be to join the King's army and defeat the wiles of Satan: not just to escape hell! As we study the word of God and meditate upon the Story of Calvary, we realize that indeed our salvation was extremely costly! In 1 Peter1:15, 16, 18, 19 we have these inspired words: "As He which has called you is Holy, so be ye holy in all manner of conversation, because it is written, 'Be ye Holy: for I am Holy.' For as much as ye were not redeemed with corruptible things, as silver and gold, from your vain conversation received by tradition from your fathers. But with the precious blood of Christ as a lamb without blemish and without spot."

Remember, we have been delivered from the power of darkness and translated into the Kingdom of His Dear Son. (Colossians 1:13.) Unlike the earthly process which does not allow an alien to be immediately naturalized, God immediately raises us up out of Satan's kingdom and positions us in heavenly places in Christ Jesus.

    b.   *The successful applicant must take a pledge of allegiance to respect and honour the laws of his new country.*

Naturalization, however, is not automatic. According to Ephesians 2:12, before our conversion, we were aliens from the Commonwealth of Israel. In conformity with the law, both temporal and heavenly, an alien cannot be granted naturalization immediately upon request. However, through Abraham, the father of us all, provision has been made for our immediate entrance into the Kingdom of God through the futuristic revelation of the efficacy of the blood of Jesus Christ, our Redeemer.

Among His many promises made to Abraham, God promised him that through him ALL families of the earth would be blest. (Acts 3:25,26.) Romans 4:11 reads "And he (Abraham) received the sign of circumcision, a seal of the righteousness of faith which he had yet being uncircumcised: that he might be the father of all them that believe, though they be not circumcised; that righteousness might be imputed unto them also." Further Galatians 3:7 states "Know ye therefore that they which are of faith, the same are the children of Abraham?"

In fact, Abram's name was changed to Abraham which means 'father of many nations'. God was extremely proud of His servant Abraham and called him 'His friend.' God highly honoured this friendship in so much that as Genesis 15:18 records, His promises to Abraham were confirmed by sacrifices and became a covenant. It is through this covenant that we are granted the privilege to become naturalized citizens of The Kingdom of God.

c. <u>Amnesty</u>

What is an amnesty?

Amnesty is defined as a general pardon given by a government to prisoners, outlaws, or rebels. It is derived from the Greek *"amnestia"*, which is translated *"to forget."*

In an article published by US Conservative politics, Justin Quinn defines amnesty as any Governmental pardon for past offences or crimes, especially political ones. Granting an amnesty goes far beyond a pardon in that, it forgives the offender completely, and is usually associated with granting the offender freedom from deportation and even capital punishment.

When I realized the awesomeness of this definition, I felt like shouting, jumping, skipping, and dancing. I was overwhelmed. Ephesians 2: 12 says that (referring to the time before we were saved,) we were without Christ, being aliens from the Commonwealth of Israel, (not of the seed of Abraham), strangers from the covenant of promise having no hope, and without God in the world. We had no immigration status to enter into the Kingdom of God.

We were also doomed to receive the death penalty. Psalm 14:2 says The Lord looked down from heaven upon the children of men, to see if there were any that did understand, and seek God. They are all gone aside, they are altogether become filthy: there is none that doeth good, no, not one.

All have sinned. In Romans 5 we are told that sin reigned from Adam to Moses even over them that did not sin after the similitude of Adam's transgression. Sin brought death into the world: for the wages of sin is death commonly called capital punishment when recommended by a Government. *(Taken from Scripture to support Amnesty from Thoughts of Robert Glenn Paratten.)*

Unlike Naturalization, an Amnesty is an act that by passes all the 'red tape' and comes into effect immediately. The petition "Thy Kingdom Come" admonishes believers to request that inner kingdom: the attainment of a personal salvation, a moral and psychological condition based upon the proclamation of Our Lord Jesus to a mixed multitude in St. Luke 17:21.

The Kingdom of God is within you

In Philippians 2:12, 13, St. Paul admonishes us as saints of God to work out our own salvation with fear and trembling. God is already working in us both to will and to do of His good pleasure. This "working out" can only be accomplished if the souls of the saints are in a state of piety and humility; a soul over which God reigns supreme.

Jesus knew the tribulations that future saints would have to endure, so He bids us to daily ask for a swift arrival of the Day of

The Lord: a state in which all creation will be completely under the control of God.

* * * * * *

PETITION 2:

THY WILL BE DONE ON EARTH AS IT IS IN HEAVEN.

Corresponding verses

(a) *I delight to do Thy Will O my God. Psalm 40: 8*

(b) *That ye may stand perfect and complete in all the will of God. Colossians 4:12*

At a very early age, the Lord Jesus demonstrated that He came to do His Father's will, the will of Him that sent Him. When His parents sought Him anxiously for three days in Jerusalem after the Feast of the Passover, He said unto them, *"Why do you seek Me? Did you not know that I must be about My Father's business?"*

I believe that during His first twelve years spent with His earthly parents, Jesus tried to convince them that the real reason why He came to earth was to do the will of His Father. Therefore, He was surprised when His mother searched among the crowd for Him for three days instead of coming directly to the Temple to look for Him.

Jesus did not engage in social conversations with His family members and friends after the feast. His parents found Him in God's house actively engaged in God's word. I really think that perhaps He missed the sweet communion He had with the Father before He came to earth and believed that the best place to go was to the House of God. Perhaps He was questioning them about the first Feast of the Passover. After all He was with the Father when the feast was instituted and the death angel destroyed the first born among the Egyptians.

Although Jesus' visit to the temple happened about eighteen years before He began His earthly ministry, I believe Nicodemus (the man who came to Jesus by night in search of salvation), was among the doctors and lawyers in the Temple at that time. Mary and Joseph looked for the Lord Jesus and found Him. Nicodemus also found Him. What about you? Are you looking for Our Lord and Saviour Jesus Christ? I am reminded of a popular Spiritual that says 'Everybody ought to know who Jesus is'. Do you know who Jesus Is?

Several years later, one day as He spoke to the multitude, Jesus said, *"I am The Way, The Truth, and The Life: no man cometh unto the Father but by Me." St. John 14:6.* Are you looking for the Saviour of the whole world in the right places? Do you read the word of God? Perhaps a good place to begin is at St. John's Gospel chapter 3 and then Romans chapter 8.

At another time the Lord Jesus said, "Search the Scriptures; for in them ye think ye have eternal life; and they are they; which testify of Me." St. John 5:39.

Do we attend The House of God and actively engage our minds on the word of God as it is preached by sincere men of God? Do we give earnest heed to the Word of the One who came to do The Father's will? Jesus knew that He had a limited time to do God's will. Let us adopt this attitude and agree with King David who, as he escaped from

King Saul, said to Ahimelech, "The King's business requires haste." 1Samuel 21:8.

In this prayer, the Way of Salvation is not 'spelled out', But Jesus who came from the bosom of the Father was cognizant that it was the Father's will that none should perish; He knew that St. John 3:16 was at the centre of the will of His Father.

One day as He spoke to a mixed multitude, (including the unbelieving Jews), He said, "And this is the will of Him that sent Me, that everyone which sees the Son, and believes on Him, may have everlasting life: and I will raise him up at the last day." St. John 6:40.

When our Redeemer introduced the term 'Thy will be done' in this model prayer, He included in essence, His conversation with Nicodemus which was practically consummated at Calvary.

In the Garden of Gethsemane, as He was about to suffer for the sins of the whole world; past, present, and future, our Saviour submitted Himself to the Father's will although He dreaded the hour when He would be forsaken by His Loving Father: the God who had never left Him. St. Luke 22:41-42, And He was withdrawn from them about a stone's cast, and kneeled down and prayed saying "Father, if thou be willing remove this cup from me: nevertheless, not my will, but Thine be done." St. Matthew records that He went away the third time and spoke the same words.

Exuberant in Spirit, although His body was wracked with pain; His last two words on the cross of Calvary were "It is finished", and "Father into Thy hands I commit my Spirit." The will of His Father during His earthly ministry had been accomplished. Hallelujah! His one passionate desire as recorded in the greater part of the Holy

Scriptures was to do the will of the Father.

Many, many years before in Psalm 40:7, King David prophesied the Lord Jesus as saying, "Lo, I come in the volume of the Book it is written of Me, I delight to do Thy Will O my God, yea, Thy law is within my heart." This passage is also recorded in the New Testament, Hebrews 10:7.

Our Lord and Saviour, Jesus Christ was worthy to be accepted by His Heavenly Father: never to be separated from Him again. It is no small wonder that jubilant alleluias rang out all through the portals of God's celestial city as seraphim and cherubim welcomed home the Son of God at His victorious and glorious resurrection. Under the Power of the Holy Spirit, the sweet Psalmist of Israel describes this memorable occasion in Psalm 24.

Because of His commitment to His Father, His determination to do the Father's will, and His everlasting love for mankind, my Savior, the Lord Jesus Christ is long suffering to us all, not willing that any should perish, but that all should come to repentance.

* * * * * * *

PETITION 3:

GIVE US THIS DAY OUR DAILY BREAD.

Corresponding verses

(a) *What is 'Our Daily Bread'?*

(b) *I am the Bread of Life. St. John 6:48*

What is 'Our Daily Bread'?

Bread has many definitions: the most significant being, a food made from mixing flour with other ingredients, which are kneaded and baked. Bread is also defined as food in general, as well as a livelihood. Upon Adam's expulsion from the Garden of Eden, because of his disobedience, God told him that by the sweat of his face he shall eat bread.

Therefore; it may be surprising to many of us that here in this modeled prayer, Jesus, God's Beloved Son, who repeatedly said, that He came to do His Father's will, includes the petition: GIVE US THIS DAY OUR DAILY BREAD. To some of us, especially to those who do not believe in the unity of the Godhead, this may seem like a demand coming from Jesus Himself without any regard for the Father. Far be that thought. Our Lord Jesus is telling His disciples, and by extension us (the other sheep that were not of His fold at time) to expect all good things from our Heavenly Father who gives to all men liberally.   As this article progresses, I will endeavour through the inspiration of the Holy Spirit, and by the grace of God to humbly explain this statement.

To this end, there are two applications that I would like to emphasize.   Firstly, Our Lord Jesus was instructing a special set of people; His disciples. No doubt, included in His audience, were the seventy plus evangelists whom He later sent out into the surrounding regions with the good news of the Kingdom of God. His twelve disciples were also a part of this great company.

In St. Matthew 6: 28-34, Jesus told this multitude that our Heavenly Father knows exactly what we need and will provide for us. In fact, God knew everything about us before we were created. He has totally committed Himself to us. Just as a caring earthly father provides for his children, as long as we accept and acknowledge Him as our Heavenly Father, Jehovah Jireh will provide all that we need.

According to the New King James Version of Nelson's Study Bible, the multitude to whom this sermon, commonly called the Sermon on the Mount, was preached was comprised of 'children of the kingdom'. This lengthy discourse consisted of instructions for those who had responded to Jesus' invitation to repent.

What a great privilege Our Lord Jesus is affording us in this imperative sentence! It seems as if we are demanding God to immediately do as we say. However, Jesus was certain that the people in this multitude, who were His true followers, were not only hearers of the Word. He knew that for the most part they had committed themselves to doing the will of their Heavenly Father. He also knew that because of His great love for us, our heavenly Father would continue to provide for our physical and spiritual needs daily even when we fail to trust Him and same way He 'rained' down 'bread' (manna) from heaven for the Children of Israel He will certainly rain down blessing from heaven daily on all who accept His Dear Son, my Lord and Saviour Jesus Christ as the True Bread from heaven

I am certain that there are many of us who experience our Father God providing for us moment by moment. All he requires of us is that we simply trust and obey Him. What blessed assurance we have in the following words based on St. John 3:16.

For God - The greatest being

So loved - The greatest love

The world - The greatest company

That He gave - The greatest gift

His only begotten Son - The Greatest sacrifice

That whosoever believeth in Him - The simplest act

Should not perish - The greatest escape

But have everlasting life - The greatest security.

My second application is based on 'bread' in reference to St. John chapter 6. On this occasion The Saviour of the World was speaking to an entirely different audience, although I believe many of His true followers were there. However, there were also the unsaved Gentiles who were referred to as 'dogs' at that time. They did not have a Heavenly Father and were anxious about how they would obtain their daily provisions. There were the unbelieving religious Jews who sought to kill him because of the miracles that He performed; especially at that time; He had recently healed a crippled man at the Pool of Bethesda on the Sabbath Day. Then there were the lazy ones: those who were only interested in Him and wanted to make Him their King because he had just filled their stomachs with food. Finally, there were the Jewish intellectuals (or who thought they were): Scribes, Pharisees, Sadducees, and Herodians who followed Him or sent spies to trap Him as He spoke. To this mixed multitude Jesus referred to

Himself as the Bread of Life.

In Clarkes' Commentary on the Bible, this theologian refers to "our daily bread" as the supply of grace which our soul requires daily to keep it in good health and vigour. He explains that God is the author and dispenser of temporal, as well as spiritual food. The unbeliever is unable to do anything that will merit any good thing from God. Therefore, he/she must accept The Bread of Life as a free gift from God.

I am the Bread of Life St. John 6:48

St. John 6: 35 says "Jesus said unto them, I am the Bread of Life: he that cometh to Me shall never hunger: and he that believeth on Me shall never thirst." Just as God "rained" down "bread" (manna) from heaven for The Children of Israel, He will certainly 'rain down blessings from heaven daily on all who accept His Dear Son, Our Loving Lord and Saviour, Jesus Christ, as the True Bread from heaven.

In St. John 6:30 -33 we read "They (the multitude), said therefore unto Him, What sign shewest thou then, that we may see, and believe Thee? What dost Thou work? Our fathers did eat manna in the desert, as it is written, 'He gave them bread from heaven to eat'. Then said Jesus unto them, "Verily, verily, I say unto you, Moses gave you not that bread from heaven, but my father giveth you the true bread from heaven. For the bread of God is He which cometh down from heaven, and giveth life unto the world."

In referring to the people's comment that Moses gave them

bread from heaven, Jesus informed them that, that bread did not come from Moses. In other words, He was saying that God provided that which Moses called 'bread'.

Was this a divine revelation given to Moses that manna was a type of the Lord Jesus, whom God would one day send to the earth? Was Moses by divine inspiration referring to the coming of the Lord Jesus as the 'True Bread' from heaven?

Jesus reminded the mixed multitude, that although that bread came from heaven, where God reigns supreme, it did not sustain their forefathers forever: they are no longer alive. The time had not yet come when God would send that true bread from heaven. In fact, because of their ingratitude and lack of appreciation of what He had already provided for them as He led them out of the land of Egypt they had a long way to go.

Many generations would pass before they would practically behold the True Bread from heaven. However, the omniscient God knew that even when that time came many of the Jews, His chosen people would not accept the Lord Jesus, the executor of the Father's will. But, now the hour had come; the True Bread was among them in the person of our Redeemer and Saviour, the Lord Jesus Christ. St. John 6:35, And Jesus said unto them, "I am the bread of life: he that cometh to Me shall never hunger; and he that believeth in Me, shall never thirst."

Recently, in a conversation with the Samaritan Woman at Sychar's well, Jesus had told her that whosoever drinks the water that He gives will never thirst because the water that he gives is a fountain springing up into eternal life. The following verses, found in verses 13 & 14 of St. John chapter 4 quotes exactly what Jesus said to her -

"Jesus answered and said unto her, "Whosoever drinketh of this water shall thirst again. But whosoever drinketh of the water that I shall give him shall never thirst; but the water that I shall give him shall be in him a well of water springing up into everlasting life."

The Samaritan woman believed on Him and because of her testimony, many people in Samaria believed also, and received eternal life. However, the religious Jews in this company were different. They continued to argue among themselves, and with the Lord Jesus. Sad to say, but many of them, including His followers, rejected Him after this lengthy discourse.

This was around the time of the yearly feast of Tabernacles at Jerusalem and no doubt, many people were travelling up to Jerusalem for that occasion. Also many in the towns and villages nearby had heard of the miraculous feeding of the multitudes and were seeking the Lord Jesus to obtain 'free food'! These included Jews as well as Gentiles.

Our Saviour Jesus Christ used this opportunity, which was of course already in the plan of His Heavenly Father, to inform peoples of all nations that El Shaddai was also presenting to them the gift of salvation; they were invited to partake of the Bread of Life. In fact, the feeding of two large multitudes: the Feeding of the 5,000 and the Feeding of the 4,000 are recorded in the Gospels of St. Matthew and St. Mark. (*St. Mark was also known as John Mark. John was his Jewish name and Mark was his Roman name. Bible scholars agree that he spent much time in Rome with St. Paul during his imprisonment in that city; hence the reason to believe that Mark wrote for both Jewish and Gentile audiences more so than St. Matthew.* **Ancient Faith Program**)

Therefore, when John Mark wrote his Gospel, he had no

problem with Jesus including the blessing of God toward Gentile nations. For example, Mark records that Jesus sent the twelve apostles into all cities with the Gospel. Matthew, in spite of some concern for the Gentiles, makes special mention of Jesus telling the apostles to go only to the lost tribes of Israel.

A Biblical scholar on the *Ancient Faith program*, records that he believes that since Jesus took time out to discuss these miracles with His disciples, the feeding of the 5,000 was mainly for the Jews to understand that the Bread of Life had come to them because of the use of the number twelve. "They took up twelve baskets full of the fragments, and of the fishes." St. Mark 6:43. This was a popular number among the Jews: twelve tribes of Israel, twelve disciples, twelve Apostles, excluding St. Paul who wrote to the Church at Corinth as well as to all saints in every place, the following exhortation. "And last of all He was seen of me also, as one born out of due time. For I am the least of the apostles, that am not meet to be called an apostle." I Corinthians 15:8-9. Later through Divine revelation, the writer of St. John's gospel saw twelve significant parts of the infrastructure of the New Jerusalem as it descended from heaven: examples were twelve foundations, twelve gates, and twelve precious stones.

In the recording of the Feeding of the 4,000, seven baskets are left over: seven being a symbol of fullness and completion: thus including God's ability to provide for his entire creation. "So they did eat, and were filled: and they took up of the broken meat that was left seven baskets." St. Mark 8:8. In other words, Jesus is the Living Bread sent by God the Father to provide for the physical and spiritual the needs of the entire world: Jew and Gentile alike.

Under the unction of the Holy Spirit, The Feeding of the 5,000 is the only miracle that is recorded in the four Gospels: St. Matthew,

St. Mark, St. Luke, and St. John. During my fifty-plus years teaching in secular and religious institutions, I have known it to be the favourite miracle among primary or elementary students. Probably, this is because a picnic setting, and a young child's lunch and are involved.

However, you must remember that although God in His mercy provides for His entire creation, the time is drawing near when those of us on this terrestrial ball, who do accept the Saviour of this world as the True Bread from heaven, will not enter into the celestial New Jerusalem.

* * * * * * *

PETITION 4:

FORGIVE US OUR DEBTS AS WE FORGIVE OUR DEBTORS.

Corresponding verses

(a) *Who can forgive sins, but God only? Mark 2:7*

(b) *The Son of Man hath power on earth to forgive sins. Mark 2:10*

Since our heavenly Father, the Lord God Almighty, El Elyon, the Creator of the universe, made provision from the beginning of time, for those of us who deliberately trespassed against Him to seek his forgiveness, shouldn't we, His undeserving creatures, obey the words of His Beloved Son, our Lord and Saviour, Jesus Christ and forgive those who trespass against us?

God the Father went to the extreme to save the Kingdom of Israel when He gave the prophet Hosea the model prayer mentioned in Hosea 14:6-7. However, He went to uttermost extremity, when He displayed His boundless love for us, an undeserving race, and gave His only begotten Son who left the splendors of Heaven, the portals of Glory, and the bosom of His Heavenly Father to give us the unspeakable privilege to seek God's forgiveness. Once again I repeat for emphasis: shouldn't we, His undeserving creatures, obey the words of His Beloved Son, our Lord and Saviour Jesus Christ and forgive those who trespass against us? In St. Matthew 6:14-15 Jesus says "For if ye forgive men their trespasses your heavenly Father will also forgive you. But if ye forgive not men their trespasses, neither will your Father forgive your trespasses." Psalm 86:5 says "For thou Lord art good, and ready to forgive, and plenteous in mercy unto all them that call upon Thee."

In the parable of The Unforgiving Servant recorded in St. Matthew 18:23-35, the Lord Jesus said to the Apostle Peter, that if we do not forgive from our heart, we will be in danger of God treating us as one of the king's chief servants treated his fellow servant. In concluding the parable, our forgiving Saviour quoted "So likewise shall my heavenly Father do also unto you, if you from your hearts forgive not everyone his brother their trespasses, St. Matthew 18:35."

In St. Mark 11:24-26, Jesus states that forgiving others is closely associated with having God answer our prayers. "Therefore, I say unto you, whatsoever thing ye desire, when you pray, believe that ye receive them and ye shall have them. Verse 25, and when ye stand praying, forgive if ye have ought against any, that your heavenly Father also which is in heaven, may forgive you your trespasses. But ye do not forgive, neither will your Father which is in heaven forgive your trespasses."

In St. Luke 23:24, Jesus prayed for them that despised and cruelly treated Him during His crucifixion. He said," Father forgive them: they know not what they do."

In writing to the local church at Corinth, St. Paul the Apostle, admonished the saints to forgive the brother who repented of his adultery; to be gracious unto him and to confirm their love for him as he was extended the right hand of fellowship among them once again. This admonition is also applicable to Bible-believing saints today. The importance of forgiveness is recommended by the Divinely inspired writers of the Torah, the Prophecies (including the Psalms), the Gospels, The Acts of the Apostles, and the Epistles. However, forgiving others is only possible if we have a pure heart. Let us not think about what others may have done adversely to us. When we refuse to forgive others, we are regarding iniquity in our hearts. Psalm 66:18 says that if we regard iniquity in our heart the Lord will not hear us. As Christians, we are totally dependent upon God and we cannot afford for Him to turn a deaf ear toward us. This is an absolutely serious matter! So is obeying all of God's commands in His Holy inspired word. Selah.

It is true that 'it rains on the just, as well as the unjust'. And in His Sovereign mercy, God cares for His entire creation; this includes both animals and plants. But the blessing of the Lord is with them that fear Him. Therefore, those of us who fear God enjoys His sovereign mercies as well as His blessings. Psalm 32:1 reads "Blessed is he whose transgression is forgiven, whose sin is covered. Blessed is the man unto whom the Lord imputeth not iniquity, and in whose spirit there is no guile."

We cannot audibly hear the words of the Lord Jesus as He said to the paralyzed man - "Son be of good cheer; thy sins are forgiven thee"

(Matthew 9:2); but my dear reader, if you are not born again, the precious words of this consoling message spoken by my Saviour to the paralytic man by the grace of God, also applies to you if you avail yourself of it. May you express faith in the Lord Jesus for your salvation as I did, and also the friends of the palsied man for his physical healing, and pray with King David in Psalm 32:5, "I acknowledge my sin unto Thee, and mine iniquity have I not hid. I said, I will confess my transgression unto the Lord; and Thou forgavest the iniquity of my sin."

If you have accepted the Lord's offer of Salvation, together with myself, through God's immeasurable grace, let us meditate on the words of Psalm 66:18- 20 which reads "If I regard iniquity in my heart the Lord will not hear me. But verily, God hath heard me; He hath attended to the voice of my prayer. Blessed be God, which hath not turn away my prayer, nor His mercy from me."

The beloved Apostle, St. John, in 1 John 1:9 records, "If we confess our sin, He is faithful and just to forgive us our sins and to cleanse us from all unrighteousness." May Our God, the God of our salvation, through the Holy Spirit, help us to appreciate the profound love of Jesus as expressed by Cecil F. Alexander, (1818-1895), in the lyrics of 'There is a Green Hill Far away', especially the following stanza:

He (Jesus) died that we might forgiven,

He died to make us good,

That we might go at last to heaven,

Saved by His precious blood.

St. Matthew 6:12, 14 states "And forgive us our debts, as we forgive our debtors. For if ye forgive men their trespasses, your heavenly Father will also forgive you."

It is of Divine significance that this portion of our Lord's modeled prayer is immediately followed by these words: 'and lead us not into temptation'. Our Omniscient Lord knows the pride that automatically arises in my heart when someone 'rubs me the wrong way'. Instead of 'counting to ten', I retaliate, and in most cases far too quickly: almost immediately I resolve in my heart to get even, or to respond in kind without thinking about the admonition that came directly from our Saviour's mouth: *as we forgive*

In fact, this is not the final section of the exposition on the Lord's prayer that I am attempting to write, through the guidance of the Holy Spirit, but it is the final one that I have chosen to be will be exposited. You see, I have been wrestling for quite a while with the thought of being unworthy to write on such a topic. I am constantly praying to my forgiving Saviour to enable me to refrain from being tempted into spontaneous retaliation when I may have been wronged unjustly, or to graciously accept an apology when it is extended to me. Therefore, firstly, this portion more than any other, is dedicated directly to myself, and secondly, to my readers of like faith that together, through the Holy Spirit, Christ may dwell in our hearts and that we may be rooted and grounded together in a love that passes all understanding and knowledge.

Like many other 'first occurrences' in the Holy Scriptures, the first record of people (Adam and Eve), being forgiven by God is in Genesis. The Divine method of forgiving sins was instituted by God Himself during the dawn of the Israelites and was given to Moses.

Whether an Israelite disobeyed the commandments deliberately, or unknowingly, he was required to confess his act of disobedience to the priest and bring a trespass offering in order to be forgiven for the sin that he had committed. The offering was divided into two parts:

one part was offered as an atonement, or reconciliation between God and himself, or simply put, asking God for forgiveness. The blood was sprinkled on the sides, and at the bottom of the altar. The entire second part of the offering was to be burned upon the altar and offered as a burnt offering for sin. This sacrifice was to be made whenever a sin was committed.

The high priest, who represented God, was commanded to make an atonement for the Children of Israel once a year. This was to be an everlasting statute or commandment. Leviticus 16:33-34 reads "And he (the priest) shall make an atonement for the holy sanctuary, and he shall make an atonement for the congregation of the tabernacle, and for the altar, and he shall make an atonement for the priests, and for all the people of the congregation. And this shall be an everlasting statute unto you, to make an atonement for the Children of Israel for all their sins once a year. And he did as the Lord commanded Moses."

Additionally, anyone in the congregation of Israel who refused to do as commanded was destroyed. Even the high priest, if he entered into the Holy of Holiest in the sanctuary unworthily, was smitten by God.

At the beginning of creation when Adam and Eve disobeyed God in the Garden of Eden, after they confessed their sin of disobedience, God made coverings of animal skins for them. Obviously, an animal was killed and consequently, blood was spilt. Leviticus 17:11 states "For the life of the flesh is in the blood: and I have given it to you upon the altar to make an atonement for your souls: for it is the blood that maketh an atonement for the soul."

This sacrifice was two-fold: It covered their physical bodies, as well as their transgression of the Law of God. Even the curses placed upon Adam and Eve in the Garden of Eden (Genesis 3:16-19), were reversed: especially the one made to Eve concerning childbirth. She was called the 'mother of all living'. The Saviour of the World came to us through natural childbirth. In fact, all of the curses placed upon this disobedient couple, worked together for the good of the human race and for the establishment of the Kingdom of God. What a compassionate God we have! In judgment He always remembers mercy.

Sincere prophets of old, identifying themselves with the people, continually lamented before God asking forgiveness for themselves and for the peoples of the kingdoms of Judah and Israel. The prophet Jeremiah devoted the entire Book of Lamentations to the acknowledgment and confession of the sins of Judah whom he called 'the virgin daughter of Zion'.

The prophet Hosea lamented over the iniquity of the ten tribes of the kingdom of Israel who were extremely wicked. They were referred to collectively as 'Ephraim' in the book written by Hosea and were the primary focus of his prophecy. Yet, in spite of his humiliating object lessons, the people did not ask God to forgive them for their idolatry, they did not repent as a nation, nor did they worship God whole-heartedly,

In Hosea 14:1-8, a forgiving God who had made an everlasting covenant with Abraham, Isaac and Jacob extends his compassionate mercy to the kingdom of Israel by divinely inspiring Hosea with a modeled prayer with which His chosen people could approach Him. In His loving kindness, His tender mercies, and His goodness, God pleaded with them to realize the futility of their ways and their dependence upon Baal. Verses 6 and 7 assured them of the forgiveness and blessings they would receive by returning to their great Deliverer.

However, they looked disdainfully upon God: They refused to accept His forgiveness. Therefore, they sealed their doom: their punishment was inevitable.

My dear reader, if you have not accepted the gift of God's forgiveness, you are in the same deplorable state. Your judgment is inevitable. God's Holy Word contains many model prayers that could be used by the Holy Spirit to lead you to an all forgiving Jesus. 2 Timothy 2:16 says "All scripture is given by inspiration of God, and is profitable for doctrine, for reproof, for correction, for instruction in righteousness."

As a born-again believer, I humbly entreat you to carefully and prayerfully read the following words taken from the Book of Hosea chapter 14 in verses 1 and 9 which read "O Israel, return unto the Lord thy God: for thou hast fallen by thine iniquity. (Verse 9) Who is wise? Let him understand these things. Who is prudent? Let him know them. For the ways of the Lord are right. The righteous walk in them. But transgressors stumble in them."

PETITION 5:

LEAD US NOT INTO TEMPTATION BUT DELIVER US FROM EVIL.

Corresponding verses

(a) *God who is faithful, will not suffer you to be tempted above that ye are able. 1 Corinthians 10:13*

(b) *The Lord our God shall deliver us. 2 Chronicles 32:11*

A casual look at this statement at first may appear to be ambiguous due to the fact "that God cannot be tempted with evil, neither tempteth He any man." James 1: 13. Perhaps a more suitable translation for temptation in 1 Corinthians could have been 'trial' or 'testing'. The following explanation is recorded from Cruden's Concordance of the Old and New Testament. (what is the year of publication?) "When spoken of God, tempt means to try or test with the idea of proving man's faith and obedience and the desire and certainty that man will not fail." Page ??

That is, God allows us to be tried or tested at times so He can prove and strengthen our faith in Him as well as our obedience to Him. His desire is that we will not fail as failure will not be to the honour and glory of His hallowed name.

Thank God for the examples given to us by Godly men of the Bible such as Abraham and Joseph. May He give us faith and assurance to say like Job "Behold, I go forward, but he is not there, and backward, but I cannot perceive Him: on the left hand where He doth work, but I cannot behold Him. He hideth Himself on the right hand that I cannot see Him: BUT He knoweth the way that I take; when He hath tried me, I shall come forth as gold." Job 33: 8-10.

When we yield to temptation, we sin against God. In Psalm 119:11 David says "Thy word have I hid in my heart that I might not sin against Thee." Not only did David hide God's word in his heart, he meditated upon it night and day: especially in the 'night watches.'

As Christians parents we take, or send our children to Sunday School or other related places where they would receive early Scriptural Education. Here they are usually admonished to commit Scripture verses to memory. As a Sunday School teacher, several decades ago, I recall my students proudly reciting their memory verses regularly in Sunday School classes and on special occasions. These children were hiding these golden texts in their hearts. However, unfortunately, as they became adults and had children of their own and in a few cases sent them to Sunday School, the word that they hid in their hearts when they were children did not surface. Probably, they did not meditate upon it as they were admonished to do when they attended adult classes and as a result there was no joy, no enthusiasm, no spiritual fulfillment and therefore no commitment to ensure that their children enjoyed the beautiful results of a successful life based on obeying God's word. Unlike David, they declined from the word that they once hid within their hearts.

As stated in the Parable of the Sower, the Soil, and the Seed, the cares of this world have smothered the Word of God assumedly in the hearts of many Christians in the Western World. When we walk in the light (of God's Word), the blood of 'The Word that was made flesh and dwelt among us' cleanses us from sin continually. But, in order to walk in the Light of God's word we must do as King David advises. We must read and meditate upon The Word day and night. Only then will we, as Christians, be able to resist the darts of the Evil One.

Even if God allows us to be tempted by the adversary, similar to the testing of Job, He will give us the strength and determination to resist the temptation. He will deliver us from evil by making a way for us to escape: He gives us the grace to overcome temptations daily.

Personally, through the grace of God, and His Divine intervention, I have been able to overcome some very sore temptations. When I look back and see the measly gratification I would have received, had I yielded, I immediately praise God for His deliverance. I would have enjoyed sin for a season perhaps only for a split second. No doubt, it would have been similar to having a candy turn into gravel while it was still in my mouth.

Yes, God does deliver. In 2 Samuel 22:2 and Psalm 18: 2 the psalmist David extols God for being his "Rock and his Deliverer". In Psalm 40:17 and 70: 5 David praises God who is his "Help and Deliverer"; and in Psalm 144:2 David blesses God who is his "High Tower and Deliverer". God delivered Moses from the River Nile; Moses and His people from being drowned in the Red Sea; Daniel from the lion's den; the Hebrew boys from the fiery furnace, King Hezekiah from King Sennacherib and the Assyrians; Paul and Silas from prison; and countless others. According to 2 Peter 2: 9 The Lord knoweth how to deliver the ungodly out of temptation and to reserve the unjust unto the Day of Judgement to be punished.

THE DOXOLOGY

The Doxology to the Model Prayer of Our Lord and Saviour, Jesus Christ

A doxology has been defined as: 'Words that express glory to God. They are usually written in the form of a song or hymn'. Doxologies are found mostly at the end of a song where the worshipper becomes overwhelmed by the Glorious Majesty of his/her Great God. Blessing and honour ascend to His Holy Name from a sincere heart that has experienced His wonderful and marvelous faithfulness and Love. The Lord Jesus concluded His modeled Prayer with the following doxology "For Thine is the Kingdom, and the Power, and the Glory forever, Amen." Short, but powerful.

This doxology embodies all that I have written in the foregoing parts of this thesis. However, kindly bear with me as I attempt to explain each tribute in this doxology that came directly from heart of The Lord Jesus. I am asking God for grace to be led by the inspiration of the Holy Spirit to do so humbly. My prayer is that this entire exposition will be to the honour, glory and praise of His great and adorable name, to the edification of saints, and where applicable, to the Salvation of those who are still not a part of His fold.

A. *For is thine is <u>The Kingdom</u>, and The Power, and The Glory.*

In this context, Webster's dictionary, defines 'kingdom' as the Spiritual Realm of God. In Collier's Dictionary, 'realm' is defined as 'a sphere or province as of knowledge, power, or influence'. In my opinion, a fitting combination of these two definitions as used in this context, would be 'a sphere over which the only True God is Omniscient and has influential Absolute Power'. In order to have a kingdom, one must have the power to control it. The Lord of Creation emphasized this tribute by proceeding it with the concept "power": thus reminding us that Our God not only possesses a Kingdom: He also possesses the power to establish and manage His Kingdom. Although it may not seem so at times, He is in full control. His power is absolute and everlasting. In fact, looking down through the corridors of time, in Isaiah 6:3, the angels are recorded as saying that the whole earth is filled with His glory. After all principalities and lesser powers have been conquered, this is the kingdom over which our Lord and Saviour Jesus Christ will reign. The hymn writer, Isaac Watts describes this beautifully in the following stanzas:

Jesus shall reign where'er the sun,

Does his successive journeys run.

His Kingdom spread from shore to shore,

'Til moons shall wax and wane no more.

People and realms of every tongue

Dwell on His love with sweetest song.

And infant voices shall proclaim

Their early blessings on his name.

B. *For Thine is the Kingdom, and the <u>Power,</u> and the Glory.*

Ultimate Power belongs unto God. Power is generally defined as 'rule, or, authority'.   However, in this context, I would like to extend this definition by adding two abstract nouns from Cruden's Concordance, these are 'might' and 'strength'.

In Deuteronomy 4:37, Moses reminded the Children of Israel that God brought them forth out of Egypt with His mighty power. In Psalm 68, David says that the God of Israel giveth strength and power unto His people. In Psalm 106: 8, he says that at the Red Sea God saved them that His mighty power may be known. In St. Matthew 10:1, Jesus sent forth His twelve disciples and endued them with His Power. "And when He had called unto Him His twelve disciples, He gave them power against unclean spirits, to cast them out, and to heal all manner of sickness and all manner of disease."

The Risen Lord Jesus assured His disciples that all power, both in heaven and on earth, is given unto Him, Matthew 28: 20. Therefore, they should not be afraid to teach and baptize all nations in the name of the Father, and of the Son, and of the Holy Ghost. However, in St. John 16:33, He informed them that they would suffer much tribulation while doing so. He told them that in this world they will have tribulation, but He also encouraged them by saying that He had overcome the world.

The writer to the Hebrews in Hebrews 9:14, tells us that through His death, Jesus destroyed the devil who had the power of death. In Revelation chapter 5, St. John the beloved disciple, sees a host of heavenly angels, the four beasts (guardians of the Throne of God), the twenty-four elders, and in fact, all creation acknowledging that power belongs to our Great God. "And every creature that is in heaven and on earth, and under the earth, and such as are in the sea, and all that are in them, heard I saying, Blessing, and honour, and glory, and power, be unto Him that sitteth upon the throne, and unto the lamb for ever and ever." Revelation 5:13.

As Christians are we contributing to the increase of the number of redeemed creatures in such a crowd, or, are we being neutral, and contributing to that number that St. John saw standing before the Great White Throne of God; those whose names were not written in The Book of Life? We can help to snatch a soul from the Lake of Fire, through our prayers and our missionary offerings even if we cannot go to a foreign country to take the Gospel. We can help to support those who go to tell lost mankind that the blood of Jesus has power to save.

> C. *For Thine is the Kingdom, and the Power, and the <u>Glory,</u> for ever and ever.*

Throughout the entire Bible the Glory of God is mentioned; in Exodus 33; 18, Moses asked God to show him His Glory. In His answer to Moses, God said that no man shall see His face and live. In St. John 1:18, through the inspiration of the Holy Spirit, the Apostle wrote that no man has seen the Father at any time. However, to Moses' request, God told him that His goodness was His glory! He told him that He would hide him in a cleft of the rock nearby, and cover him with His hand as His goodness passed by. No wonder Moses was on the mountain for forty days! Even then, it was a short time to see all of God's goodness: but with God nothing is impossible.

Are we hiding in the cleft of The Rock (Jesus) as we meditate on the mercy and goodness of God? We can depend on Our Lord Jesus to hide us in Himself as we honour Him with our whole-hearted obedience and watch His Glory pass by. May God give us the grace to say with the hymn writer Fanny Crosby:

A Wonderful Savior is Jesus my Lord.

A Wonderful Saviour to me.

He hideth my soul in the cleft of the Rock,

Where rivers of pleasure I see.

After procuring materials for the erection of the House of God at Jerusalem, King David said, "Thine O Lord, is the greatness, and the power, and the glory, and the victory, and the majesty: for all that is in the heavens and in the earth is Thine; Thine is the kingdom, O Lord, and Thou art exalted as head above all. Both riches and honour come of Thee and Thou reignest over all, and in Thine hand is power and might."   1 Chronicles 29:11, 12.

King David was a master player on the harp from his youth up, and I would like to think that this beautiful doxology was set to music. Throughout the Book of Psalms, most of which were written by King David, the sweet Psalmist of Israel, the Glory of God is mentioned at least twenty-one times according to Cruden's Concordance.

Throughout the entire Holy Bible, the Glory of God is mentioned. Jacob was awed by it as he witnessed it in a dream. Genesis 31: 17 says that he was afraid when he awoke from sleep. He had seen angels of God descending and ascending on a ladder extending from earth to heaven. The Glory of God appeared at the top of the ladder as God spoke to him.

In 1 Kings 8:10, 11, at the dedication of the Temple the Glory of the Lord descended in a cloud and filled the House of the Lord in so much that the priests could not perform their ceremonial duties. No doubt they were awe-struck as they were surrounded by the glory of God.

The Psalmist David dedicates Psalm 24 to Jesus, The King of Glory as He Enters the Celestial Portals of Heaven: especially verses 7-10 which read "Lift up your heads, O ye gates; and be lift up, ye everlasting doors; and the King of Glory shall come in. Who is this King of Glory? The Lord strong and mighty, The Lord mighty in battle. Lift up your heads, O ye gates; even lift them up, ye everlasting doors; and The King of Glory shall come in. Who is this King of Glory? The Lord of hosts, He is the King of Glory."

The prophet Isaiah saw the Glory of the Lord in a vision as seraphim worshiped God saying "Holy, Holy, Holy, is the Lord of hosts: the whole earth is full of His Glory." Isaiah 6:3. The angels praised God after the birth of our Lord was announced to the shepherds saying "Glory to God in the Highest, and on earth peace, goodwill toward men." St. Luke 2 14. In St. Mark 13:26, Jesus tells His disciples that after the tribulation, they would see the Son of Man coming in the clouds of heaven with power and great glory. Finally, in Revelation 21: 23, St. John the Divine sees the Glory of God and of The Lamb lighting Jerusalem, The Holy City.

A short hymn of praise commonly called 'The Doxology', was written by Thomas Ken in 1674. This hymn writer calls on all creation: both in heaven and on earth, to praise a Triune God, who daily loads us with all His benefits.

Praise God from whom all blessings flow,

Praise Him all creatures here below.

Praise Him above, ye heavenly hosts,

Praise Father, Son, Holy Ghost.

Psalm 117 reads "O Praise the Lord, all ye nations: praise Him all ye people. For His merciful kindness is great towards us: and the truth of the Lord endureth forever. Praise ye the Lord!" The psalmist David was so enraptured with praising the Lord that the theme of his last six psalms are all praises to a loving God who daily loads us with all his benefits. In fact, the last five psalms begin with the words "Praise ye the Lord." The final words of Psalm 150 written under the inspiration of the Holy Spirit is 'Praise ye the Lord.' Yes, everything that hath breath should praise the Lord, for He is worthy to be praised.

CONCLUSION: AMEN

What is the Spiritual Significance of the Term 'Amen'?

According to Collier's Dictionary, the term "Amen" is of Greek, Hebrew, and Latin origin. It is universally used to express approval after a prayer, and is defined as 'may it be so,' 'so be it', 'truly', or, 'verily.' In daily ordinary language or familiar conversations, it expresses strong agreement: for example, "amen to that", or simply "Amen" which is often repeated emphatically when someone agrees with a statement made by the speaker in an ordinary conversation.

According to Wikipedia, the term 'Amen' has been adopted in Christian worship as a concluding word for prayers and hymns. However, although the words 'verily' or, 'I tell you the truth', uttered by our Lord Jesus in the Gospels, are derived from 'Amen', they are in a class all by themselves. There is nothing the finite minds of humans can conceive that is worthy of our Creator's Amen. Isaiah 55:8-9 says "My thoughts are not your thoughts, neither are your ways My ways. For as the heavens are higher than the earth, so are My ways higher than your ways and My thoughts than your thoughts."

Our Lord's versions of Amen were used to introduce His topics as in His conversation with Nicodemus in St. John 3, His prophecy on the destruction of the Temple in Jerusalem, St. Matthew 24: 2, and in comparing the sins of Chorazin and Capernaum with the sinful conditions of Sodom, Tyre, and Sidon. Matthew 11:22- 23.

The use of the word 'Amen' at the end of doxologies agrees with its use at the end of our Lord's model prayer in Matthew 6:13. Its application as an ending to the angels' doxology in Revelation 7:12 shows that the heavenly hosts are greatly anticipating the coronation of our Heavenly King. They announced His coming to earth (His birth), ministered to Him after His recorded Temptation in the Wilderness, visited Him in the Garden of Gethsemane, announced His Resurrection, assured His disciples of His return to earth at His Ascension, and will accompany Him at His Second Coming.

Angels do not know when the Lord will come for His own, but they are interested in God's plan of salvation, and help in winning souls for Christ as outlined in Acts 8:26. St. Luke 15:10 tells us that "angels rejoice over one sinner that repents." Jesus said "Likewise I say unto you; that there is joy in the presence of God over one sinner that repenteth." In Revelation chapter 7, St. John the Divine, sees these angelic beings joining the four beasts, who guard the throne of God continually, and the twenty-four elders who are literally near to the throne of God, always praising and worshiping the Triune God.

Revelation 7:11, And all the angels stood about the throne, and about the elders and the four beasts, and fell down before the throne on their faces and worshiped God. Verse 12, Saying Amen: Blessing and Glory, and Wisdom, and Thanksgiving, and Honour, and Power, and Might, be unto Our God forever and ever. Amen.

Here is an occasion when the angels, the elders, and the four beasts, were so enthralled with the accomplishments of the Triune God that they began and ended their Doxology with Amen. I believed they joined the great redeemed multitude (Rev.7:9) in their Amen and continued with their own personal sevenfold Doxology as stated above in verse 12. It occurs to me that they were so anxious to present their praises to the King of kings that they could hardly wait.

Having being relieved from physical, environmental, and emotional discomforts, which we endure on this accursed earth, as part of this great multitude, in our glorified bodies we will gladly count it a special privilege to "worship" God: bowing continually at His feet. As immortal glorified beings, we will triumphantly join the Psalmist David with the words of Psalm 103:1-2, Bless the Lord, O my soul: and all that is within me, bless his Holy name. Bless the Lord, O my soul, and forget not all His benefits.

During our journey here on earth as we await the glorious return of Our Glorious Redeemer and King, let us join in the song penned by Robert Grant (1779-1838), and sing lustily, at the top of our voices to the Glory of God.

O worship the King all glorious above.

O gratefully sing, His power and His love;

Our Shield and Defender, the Ancient of Days,

Pavilioned in splendor, and girded with praise.

O tell of His Might, O sing of His grace,

Whose robe is the Light, whose canopy space.

His chariots of wrath the deep thunderclouds form,

And dark is His path on the wings of the storm.

Thy bountiful care what tongue can recite?

It breathes in the air, it shines in the light,

It streams from the hill, it descends to the plain,

And sweetly distils in the dew and the rain.

Frail children of dust, and feeble as frail,

In Thee do we trust, nor find Thee to fail;

Thy mercies how tender! How firm to the end!

Our Maker, Defender, Redeemer, and Friend!

<u>REFERENCES</u>

1. Cruden's Complete Concordance to the Old and New Testaments by Alexander Cruden. Hardcover. Hendrickson Publishers. Printed in the USA

2. The Marriage Supper of The Lamb by Dr. Ronald E. Shower; Israel My Glory: July 1991; Friends of Israel Gospel Ministry, Inc.

ABOUT THE AUTHOR

Mrs. Annaleta Elaine Swann is a veteran educator of over fifty years of experience as a trained teacher. She spent forty-five of these years as a primary educator in The Commonwealth of Bahamas teaching in schools on the western end of Grand Bahama and is now retired from active teaching. A native of The Turks and Caicos Islands, she developed a name among past students as well as their parents for her unswerving dedication to her vocation which she is convinced is an endowment from her Heavenly Father.

Mrs. Swann obtained her Teacher's Diploma from Shortwood Teacher's College in Jamaica in 1962 and her Teacher's Certificate in 1963 at the same institution. After teaching for a very short time in her homeland, Mrs. Swann left to join her husband on Grand Bahama. As she honed her craft, Mrs. Swann enrolled in and matriculated with a Bachelor of Education degree in Primary Education (1978) and a

Master of Education degree in Curriculum Planning (1980) from the University of Miami. Due to her love for science, she participated in several conferences and seminars in The Bahamas, United States of America and Canada, and became the focal point for science education among private and public elementary schools on the island. She taught exclusively in the public school system under the auspices of the Ministry of Education and finally retired in 2009.

A devout Christian and former Sunday School teacher with the Assemblies of Brethren in The Bahamas, Mrs. Swann became interested in the downward trend of Godliness among the youth of The Bahamas, and became convinced that her writing gift should be used in pointing Bahamian youth to God. In honing these skills, she has produced a number of short devotionals and meditations that have been placed in various books for the encouragement of Believers of all ages.

Mrs. Swann is the mother of six sons and grandmother of six boys and seven girls. She presently resides in Freeport on the island of Grand Bahama where she can be found, more often than not, tending to the fruiting and flowering plants in her garden.

If you liked this book, check our her other books by visiting her Author page at www.Amazon.com